More Tricks to Tunes

Learning to play the double bass is like learning to do many clever tricks with your fingers and bow.

Have you learned all of the tricks in Book 1? Now the maestro will show you the 'trickier tricks' in Book 2.

Practise each trick until you can do it neatly without looking. Try doing it with your eyes shut.

Then enjoy the tunes.

Audrey Akerman

Notes on the Low Strings

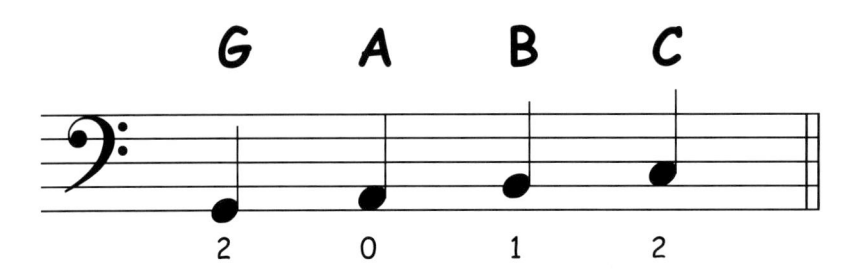

G A B C
2 0 1 2

Low **'A'** is the next string. This note is written in the bottom space of the stave.

Low **'B'** and **'C'** are fingers **1** and **2** on that string.

Low **'G'** is played with finger **2** on the lowest or **'E'** string.

Playing on the Low Strings

Play - ing on the low strings. A B C B A.

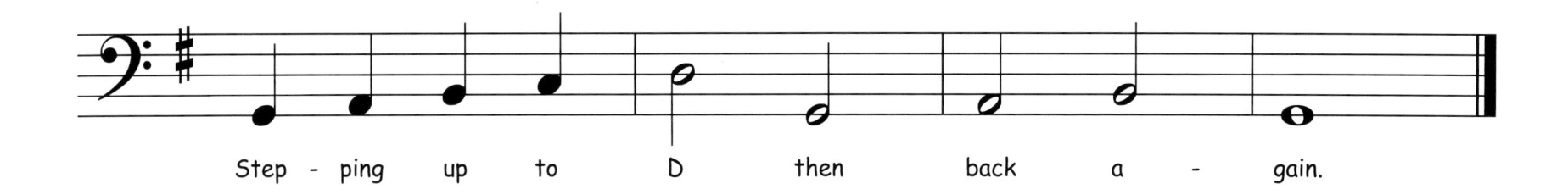

Step - ping up to D then back a - gain.

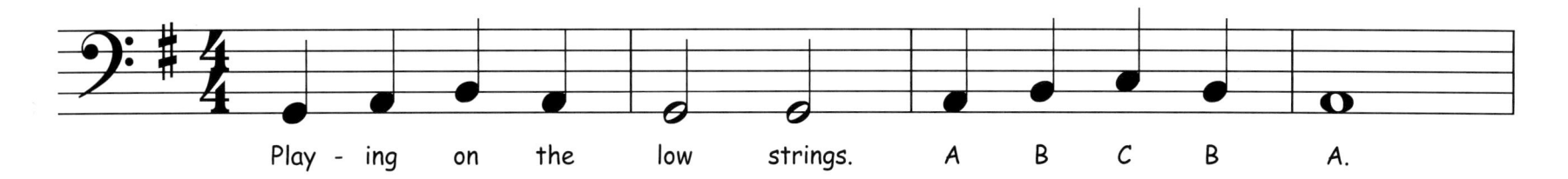

Go Tell Aunt Rhody

The Scale of 'G' Major

Start on the note **'G'** and play up 8 notes. This is the scale of **'G'** major.
Sing the names of the notes as you play them ascending.
Then do it backwards, descending.

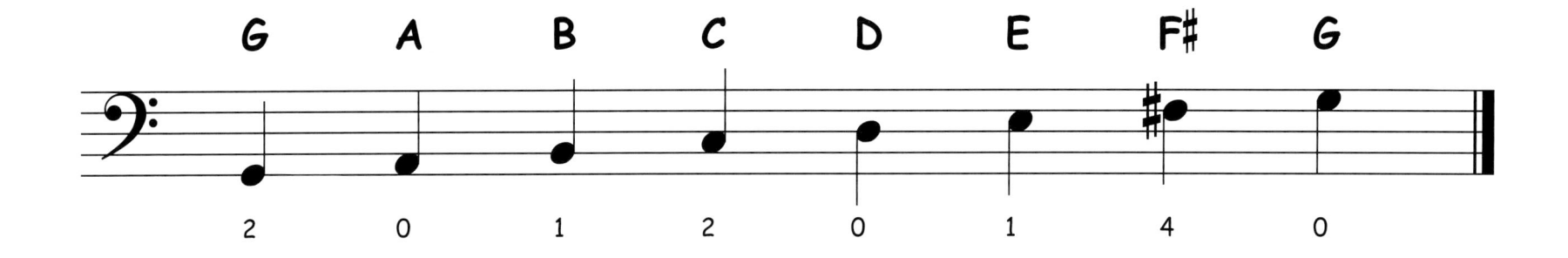

Another way of singing the scale is to use **Tonic-Solfa**.

These are the special singing names which can be used for any major scale:

Doh - Re - Mi - Fa - Soh - La - Ti - Doh

Try singing these words to your scale, ascending and descending.

1. Name each note.
    Which finger do you use to play it?

A scale is always called by the letter name of the first note.
The scale of 'G' major starts on 'G'.

2. Can you write these notes?

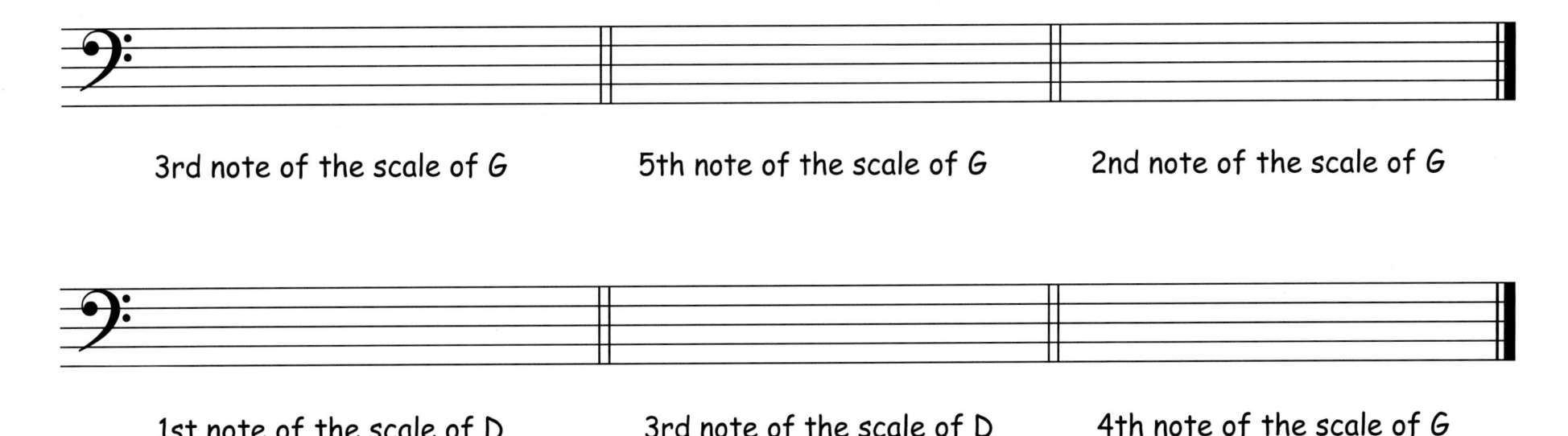

3rd note of the scale of G   5th note of the scale of G   2nd note of the scale of G

1st note of the scale of D   3rd note of the scale of D   4th note of the scale of G

Two new signs: ⊓ = down bow and ∨ = up

Sometimes we need to play two consecutive notes in the music with separate bow strokes in the same direction. The bow has to be lifted and played again for the next note.

This movement is called a **bow retake.**

Bow Tricks: Retakes

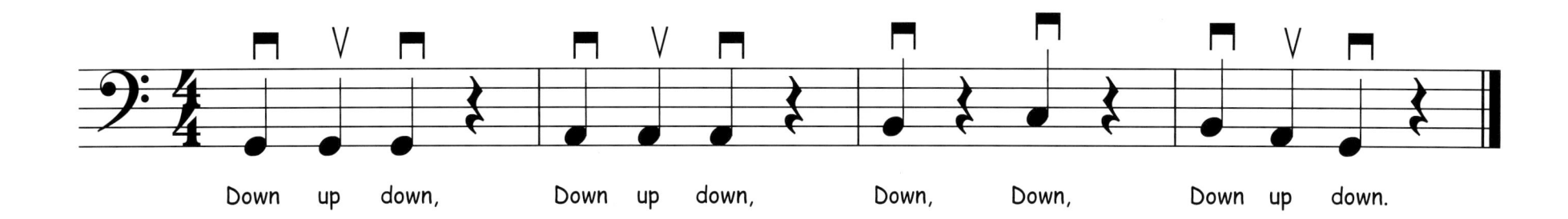

Down up down,   Down up down,   Down,   Down,   Down up down.

Au Clair de la Lune

Fine

(retake bow)

D.C. al Fine

(retake bow)

Italian words are used in music, thus making music an international language.

D stands for **Da** which means **from**.

C stands for **Capo** which means the **beginning**.

al means **to the** and **Fine** means **finish**.

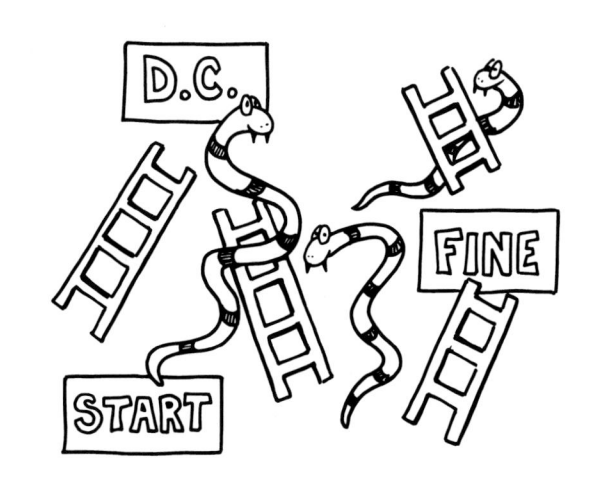

Many tunes do not start on the first beat of the bar.
This one starts on the last or 4th beat, so count 1-2-3 before you play.
The note (or notes) before the first bar line is called the
upbeat or **anacrusis.**

She'll be..........What?

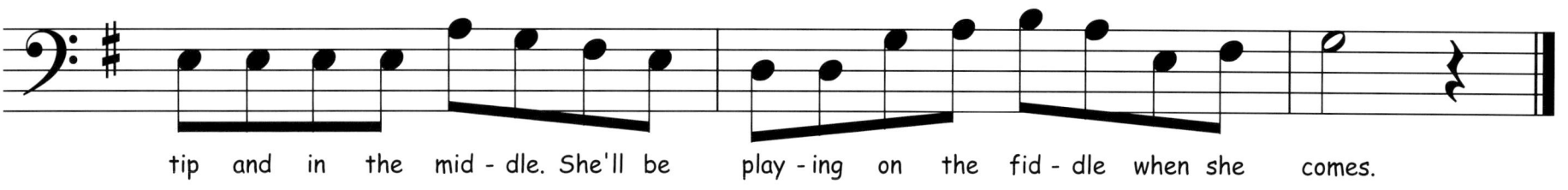

She'll be play-ing on the fid-dle when she comes. (retake) She'll be play-ing on the fid-dle when she comes. (retake) She'll be play-ing on the fid-dle. Heel and tip and in the mid-dle. She'll be play-ing on the fid-dle when she comes.

1. Put down bow signs on the first beat of each bar.

2. Remember the tune of Hot Cross Buns in Book 1?
   Can you write it in the key of 'G' major?
   The first bar is already written to help you.

Bow Tricks: Slurs

A **slur** is a curved line connecting two or more notes.
The notes joined by the slur are played with a single bow stroke.
It is like playing crotchets with your fingers while playing minims with your bow.

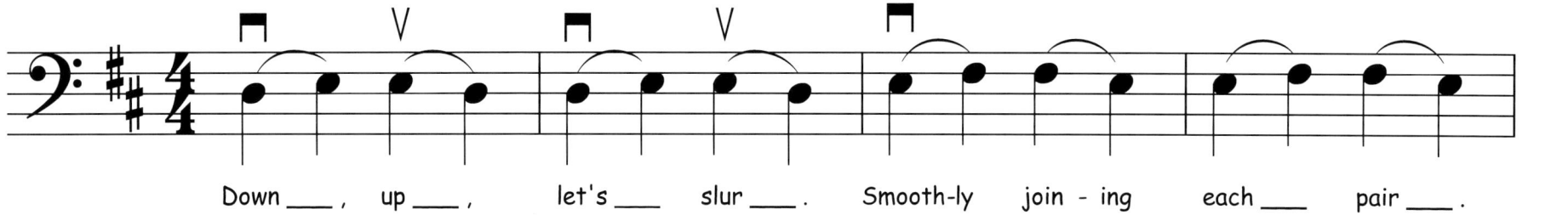

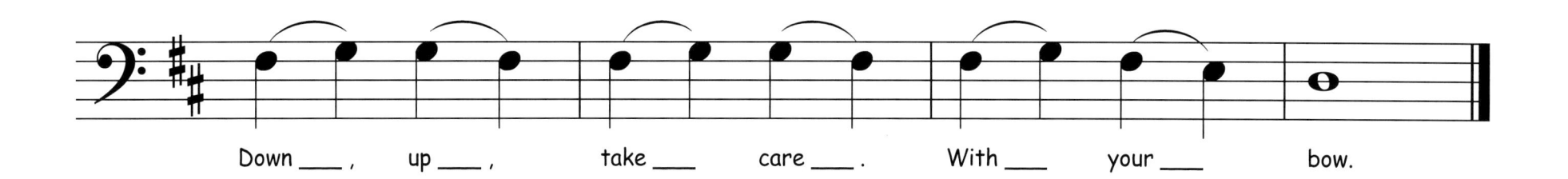

Down ___, up ___, let's ___ slur ___. Smooth-ly join - ing each ___ pair ___.

Down ___, up ___, take ___ care ___. With ___ your ___ bow.

When you have mastered this trick, try it on the other strings.

Scales with Slurs

Now try to play your scales with slurs. Play them with two notes to each bow.
Remember to play them descending (going down) as well as ascending (going up)
and sing the names of the notes as you go.

Scale of D Major   (2 Sharps)

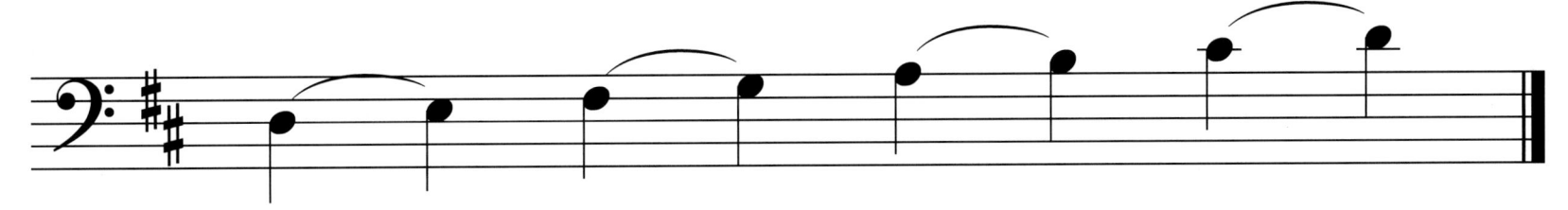

Scale of G Major   (1 Sharp)

This is a **quaver rest**.

It is a short silence, usually having **1/2 a beat**.

The note beside it, ♪ is a quaver note that is not 'holding hands'.

They always go together because you must have 2 X 1/2 beats to make 1 beat.

Over Hills and Far Away

Low C# is played with 4 fingers on the 'A' string.

Tom, he was a pip-er's son. He learnt to play when he was young. The on-ly tune that he could play, Was 'Ov-er hills and far a-way'.

1. Put in the barlines.

MUSICAL SUMS

2. Beside each group of notes write one note that has the same value.

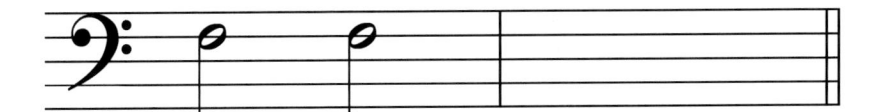

For example: ♩ + ♩ = ♪

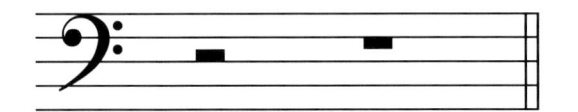

This is a **minim rest** (2 beats) and a **semibreve rest** (4 beats).
Remember: 'mini' sits and 'semi' hangs.

We now know 5 different kinds of notes and rests, and the number of beats they most commonly have.

semibreve
4 beats

dotted minim
3 beats

minim
2 beats

crotchet
1 beat

quaver
1/2 beat

More Italian Words

f stands for **forte** which means **loud**.

p stands for **piano** which means **soft**.

m stands for **mezzo** meaning **moderately**. (The word really means half in Italian.)

These words may be put together in different ways.

For example, *mf* means moderately loud, *ff* means very loud.

What do you think *pp* might mean?..

Long, Long Ago

Slurring in Threes

Slurs can join any number of notes together.

In this piece of music one bow stroke is used for each bar.

This makes it sometimes one, sometimes two and sometimes three notes for each bow.

The Giant's Lullaby

This **rest** usually has four beats.

It also means rest for a whole bar.

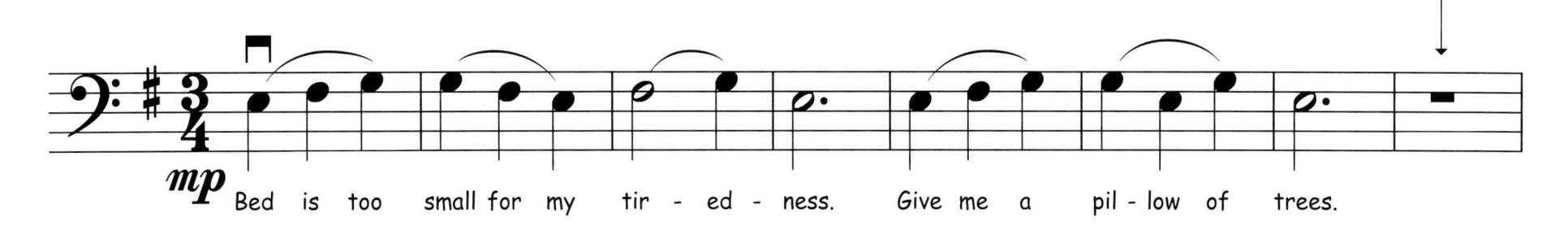

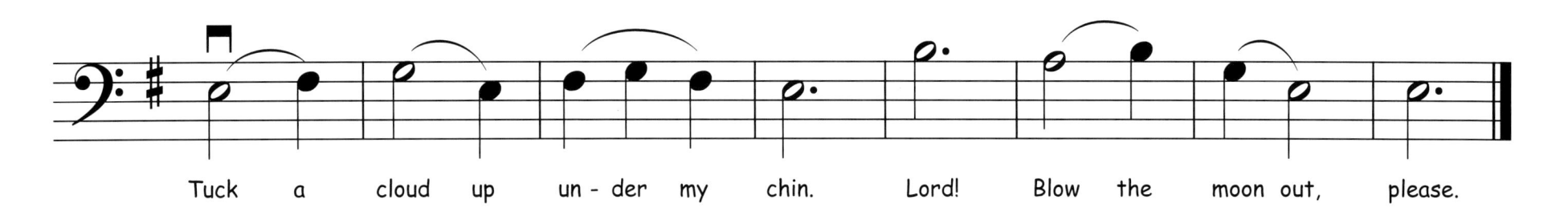

Bed is too small for my tir - ed - ness. Give me a pil - low of trees.

Tuck a cloud up un - der my chin. Lord! Blow the moon out, please.

1. Put in the barlines. Look carefully at the time signatures.

2. Beside each note write a rest of the same value.

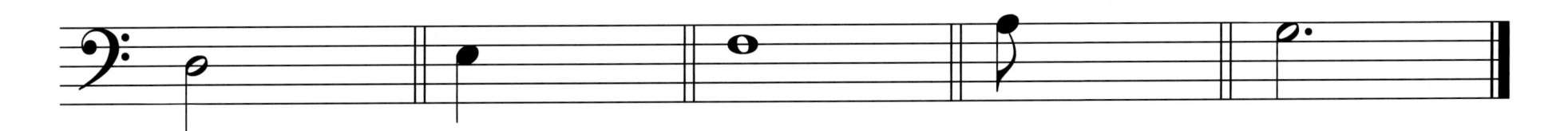

Bow Tricks: String-Crossing Slurs

Sometimes a slur joins notes which are on different strings.
The bow has to change string without changing direction.
The movement of your bowing arm will be a bit like rocking.

1. Down Bow Rocking Tricks

2. Up Bow Rocking Tricks

3. Down and Up Bow Rocking Tricks

Father's Shirt

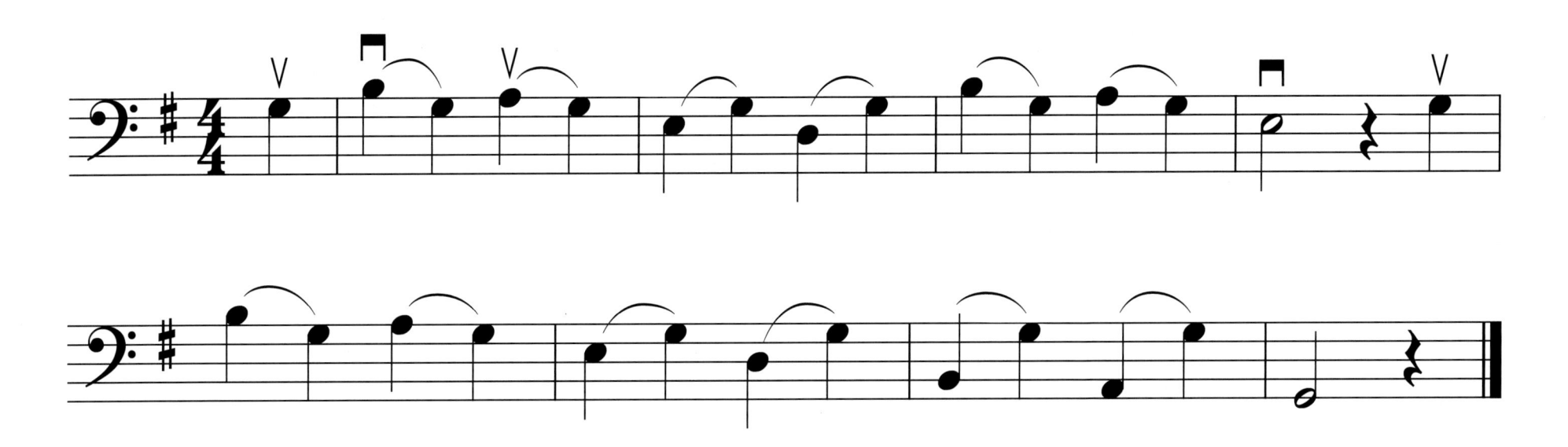

When a piece of music starts on the **anacrusis** or **upbeat** it is usual to start with an **up** bow stroke. This is so that the stronger down bow stroke will be on the first beat of the bar.

⌢ This sign is called a **fermata** and means **pause** or wait a bit.

In the Wood

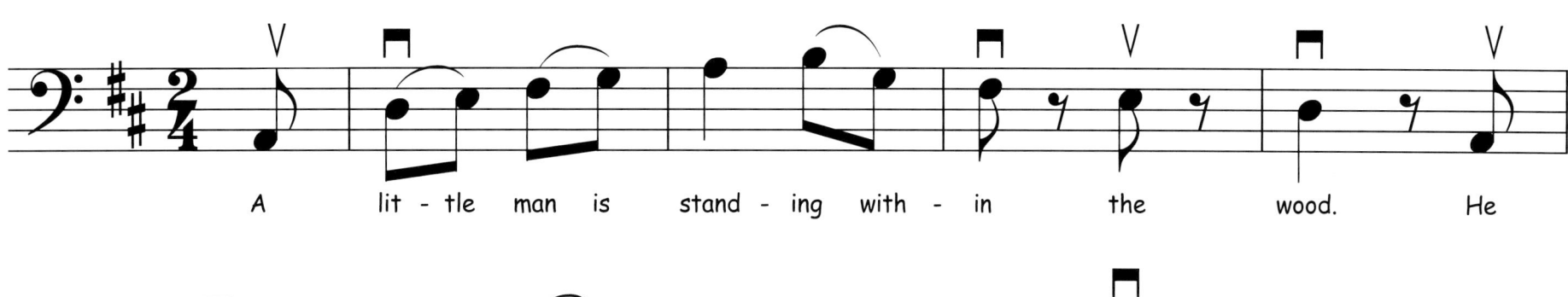

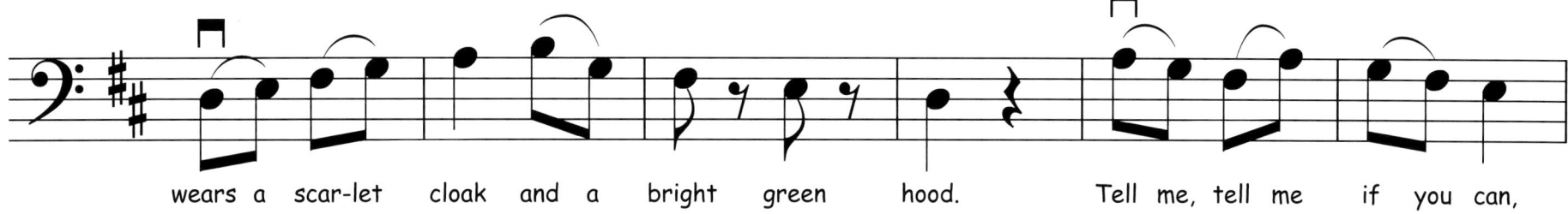

A lit-tle man is stand-ing with-in the wood. He wears a scar-let cloak and a bright green hood. Tell me, tell me if you can, Just who is this lit-tle man, Stand-ing all a-lone__ in the deep dark wood.

Answer: A Rock Orchid

1. There are too many notes in each of these bars.
   Join some of them together to make quavers so that
   there are the correct number of beats in each bar. **?**

2. Put slurs on each pair of quavers in this tune.

3. Put a rest in each bar to make the correct number of beats.

Bow Tricks: Uneven Bowing

Two beats down, one beat up

Often, when a piece of music has three beats in the bar, the rhythm has a long note for two beats and a short note for one beat.
Use a slow bow for the long note and a quicker lighter bow for the short note.

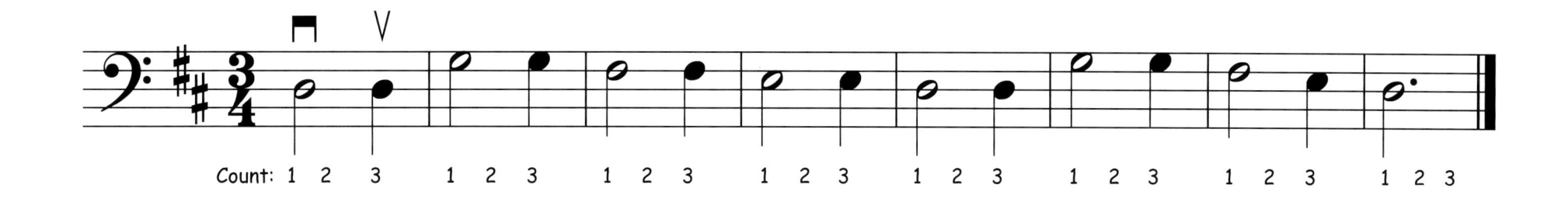

The same kind of bowing can be used with slurs.

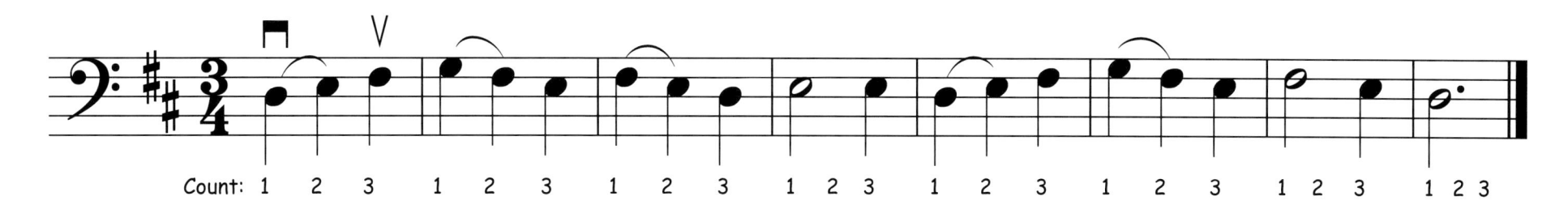

Don't forget to play the anacrusis with an up bow.

Old English Song

Polish Polka

1. This tune should be in the scale of 'D' major but the
   key signature has been left out. Put a sharp sign
   in front of each note that needs it.
   (Remember: the scale of 'D' major has two sharps, F# and C#.) ?

2. Put one note in each marked space to make the beats correct.

25

Bow Tricks: Stopped Slurs

If the slur has dots, or dashes, then it is called a **stopped slur**.
The notes joined by the slur are played with a single bow stroke which stops slightly between the notes.
It usually occurs on an up bow. It is often a repeated note.

1. Repeated note

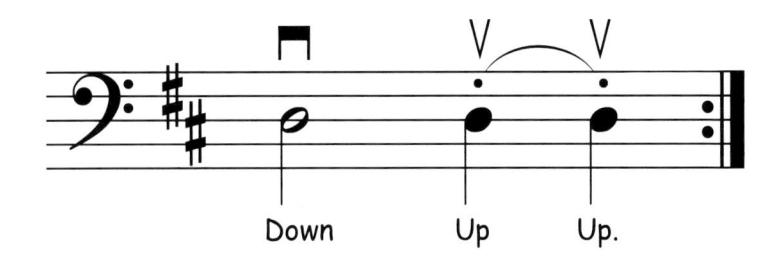

Down   Up   Up.

2. Changing note

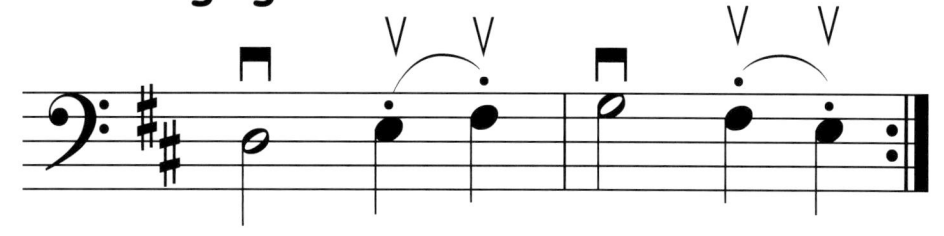

Bow Tricks: A Challenge

How many stopped slur notes can you play with one up bow?

and so on........

Clown Dance

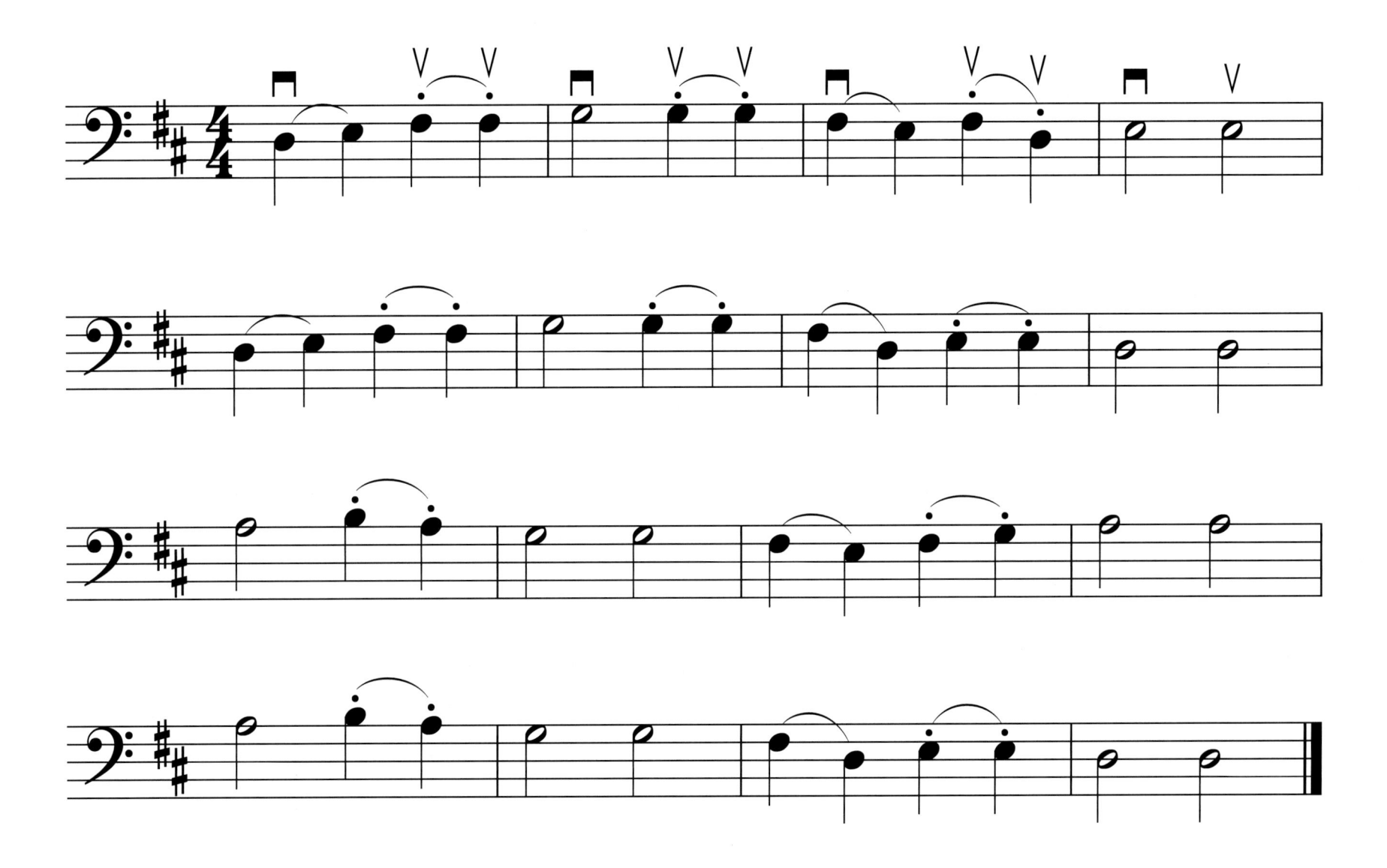

Bow Tricks: Stopped Slurs in Triple Time

Play a down bow and two short up bows in a three beat rhythm.

Down Up Up

Villikins

1. Beside each note write one that is played by the same finger one string higher. **?**

2. Put the correct time signature in each of these bars.

A New Note

This note is **'F'**.
It is written on the fourth line of the stave **without a sharp sign**.

To play this note, put two fingers on the 'D' string.

('F' is close to 'E', 'F#' is close to 'G'.)

Finger Tricks: Ministeps

Play alternately E - F - E - F - - - -

Observe:
no key signature,
so no sharps.

and so on and on and.....

A semitone is the correct music term for a **'ministep'**.
It is the distance from any note to the one immediately next to it.

A slur can join any number of notes together.
In this song the notes are sometimes slurred in '4's.

Ghosts

To play this 'ghost wail', find the highest note that you can.

mp It was ve - ry dark at ni - ght. oo - oo - oo - ooh, aa - aa - aa - aah.
Ghosts were sing - ing, out of si - ght. oo - oo - oo - ooh, aa - aa - aa - aah.
Gave us all a dread-ful fri - ght, oo - oo - oo - ooh, aa - aa - aa - aah. *pp* ooooh!

Another New Note

This note is **'C'**.
It is played by putting one finger
on the 'G' string in third position.

This is a **natural** sign.
It is used to cancel the sharp sign.

Finger Tricks: Semitones

Play alternately C# - C♮ - C# - C♮ - C# - - - -

and so on......

and so on......

The Song of the Shifting Semitones

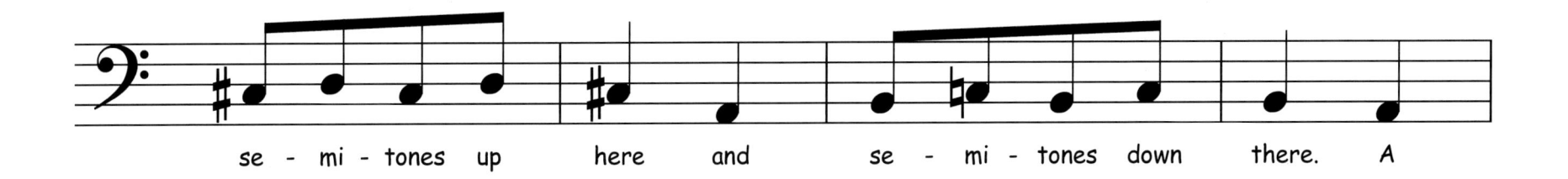

I am sharp, I am not. I can change a-bout a lot. With se-mi-tones up here and se-mi-tones down there. A sharp C next to D and not be-side a B. Sharp lot!

Kojo no Tsuki

Rentaro Taki
(1879 - 1903)

1. Write the counts for the beats under each note and rest.
   The first bar has been done to help you.

   1   2 + 3 4

2. Which of these pairs of notes is a semitone?
   Mark the semitones with an S.

35

A **fiddle** is the same as a violin. It comes from the Irish word for the violin.
To play the fiddle usually means to play folk music.

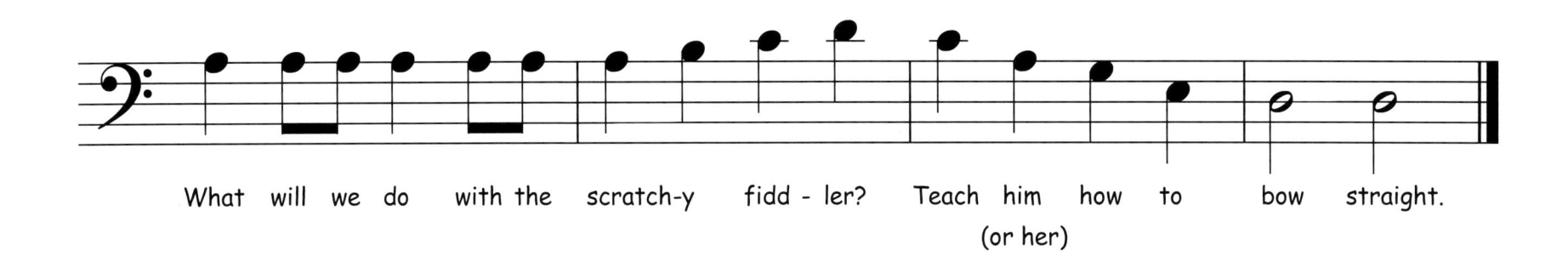

The Scratchy Fiddler

What will we do with the scratch-y fidd - ler   What will we do with the scratch-y fidd - ler,

What will we do with the scratch-y fidd - ler?   Teach him how to bow straight.
(or her)

The Scale of 'C' Major

The scale of 'C' major has no sharps.
It is the scale that uses only the white notes on the piano.
To play the top two notes of this scale move your hand up the fingerboard
to 2nd position, so that 'B' is played with finger 2 and 'C' with finger 4.

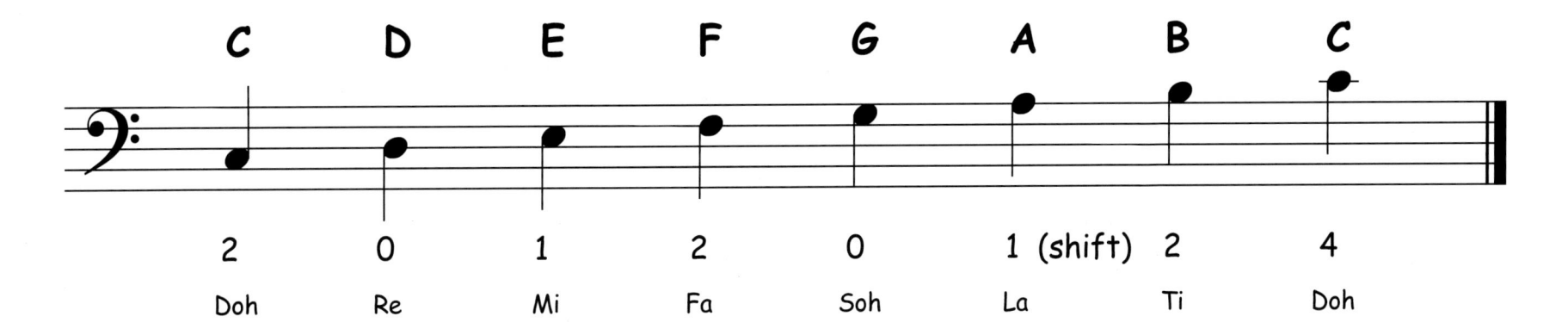

C	D	E	F	G	A	B	C
2	0	1	2	0	1 (shift)	2	4
Doh	Re	Mi	Fa	Soh	La	Ti	Doh

A major scale always has eight notes which must go in alphabetical order
from any note to the next one of the same name.
The notes always have the same distances between them:

Doh [tone] **Re** [tone] **Mi** [semitone] **Fa** [tone] **Soh** [tone] **La** [tone] **Ti** [semitone] **Doh**

A tone = 2 semitones

When a piece of music is in the scale of 'C' major, it has no key signature because it has no sharps.

C Major Twinkle

Remember the 'Twinkle Variations' in Book 1?
Try playing some of them in the scale of C major.

The word **harmony** in music means **sounding together**.

It refers to another part which can be played along with the **melody** or tune.

This is a harmony part for the C Major Twinkle. Take turns with your friends, playing the two parts together.

Twinkle Harmony

1. Write the scale of C major.
   Mark each semitone with a slur.

   ?

2. Write the following notes.

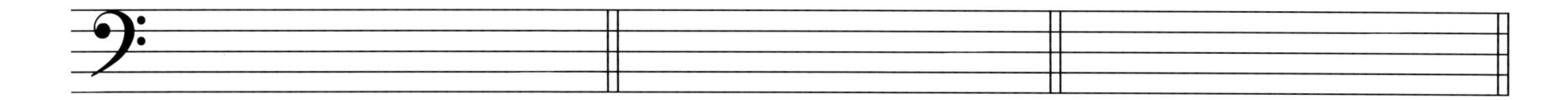

   3rd note of the scale of C   5th note of the scale of G   2nd note of the scale of D

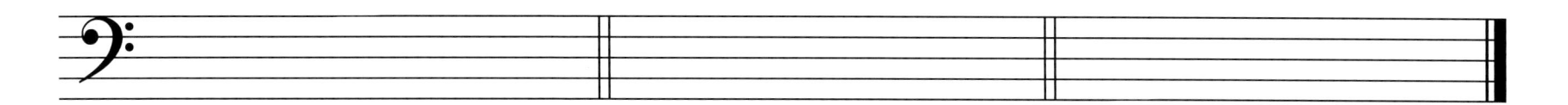

   4th note of the scale of D   6th note of the scale of C   7th note of the scale of G

The Laughing Kookaburra

The Koo-ka-bur-ra does no work. He has no work to do. His
game is on a tree to sit and cut a snake in two. And
when he's cut that snake in two he sits up-on the tree, To
Ha - Ha - Ha - Ha - Ha - Ha - Ha, Hee - Hee - Hee - Hee - Hee - Hee.

When a slur join two notes of the same pitch it is called a **tie**.
The tied note is not played seperately but is held for its full value.
By using ties it is possible to write notes of any duration.

Botany Bay

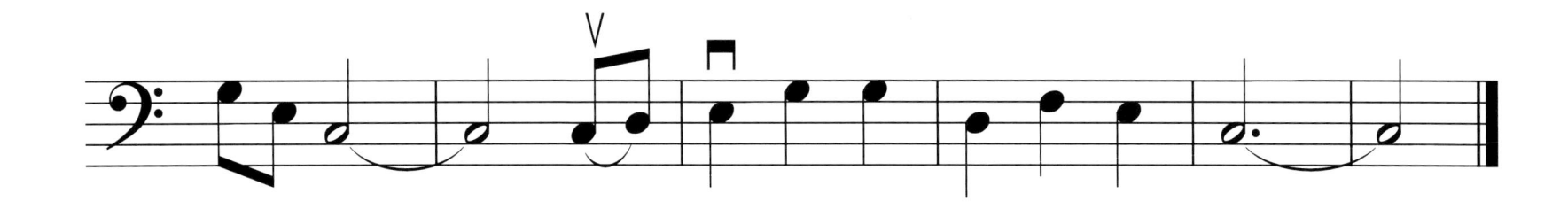

Finger Changing: Take Care

When a piece of music is in the scale of G major, F sharp is played on the 'D' string but C natural is required on the 'G' string.

Happy Birthday

Good King Wenceslas

Intervals

The gap between any two notes is called an **interval**. The distance from the first note of a scale to the second note of the scale is called the interval of a 2nd. From the first note of a scale to the fourth note of the scale is called a 4th.

1. Above each of these notes write another note to make the correct interval. The first one has been done to show you how.

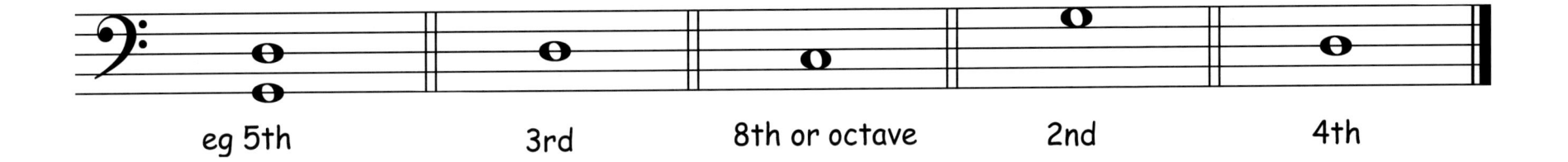

eg 5th   3rd   8th or octave   2nd   4th

2. Name the following intervals.

eg 4th

45

Bow Tricks: More Uneven Bowing

1. Use a very slow bow for the dotted minim (3 beats) and a quick light bow for the crotchet (1 beat).

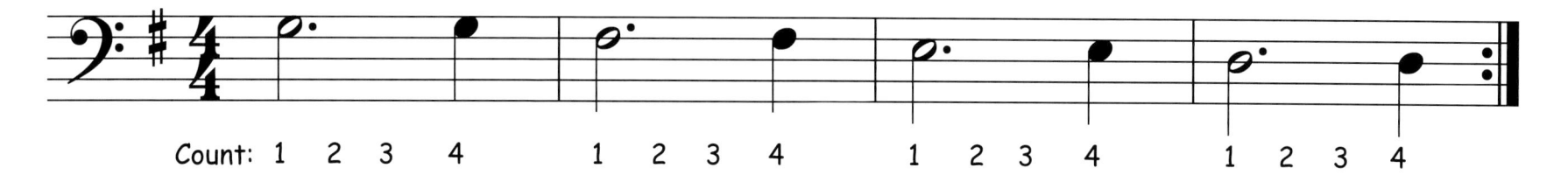

Count: 1 2 3 4   1 2 3 4   1 2 3 4   1 2 3 4

Bow Tricks: Dotted Rhythms

2. Start with a rhythm that we already know.

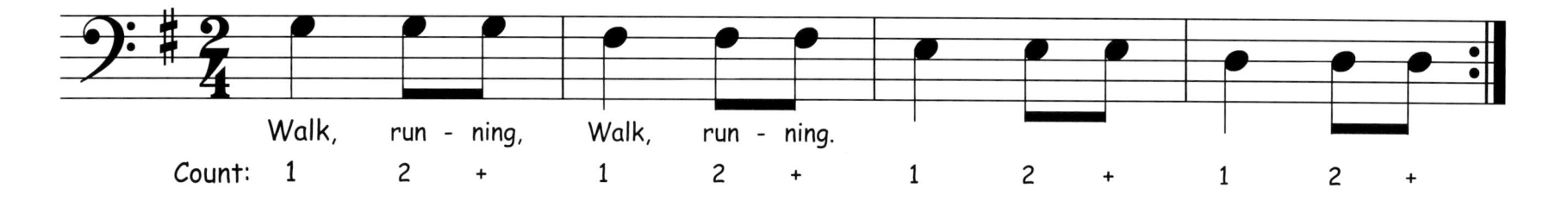

Walk, run - ning, Walk, run - ning.

Count: 1 2 +   1 2 +   1 2 +   1 2 +

3. Now try this bowing. Don't retake, just let the bow play two notes like a stopped slur, then a quick, light up bow.

4. This time, play with the first two notes tied together.

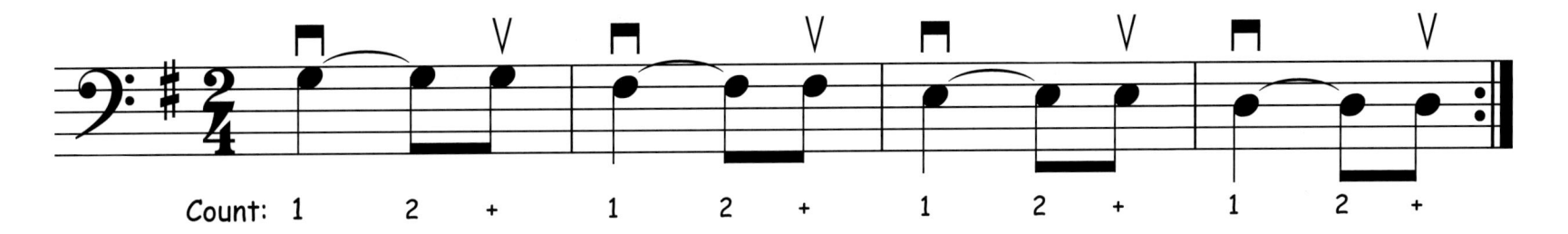

Count: 1   2   +   1   2   +   1   2   +   1   2   +

5. Another way of writing this rhythm is to use **dotted crotchets.**

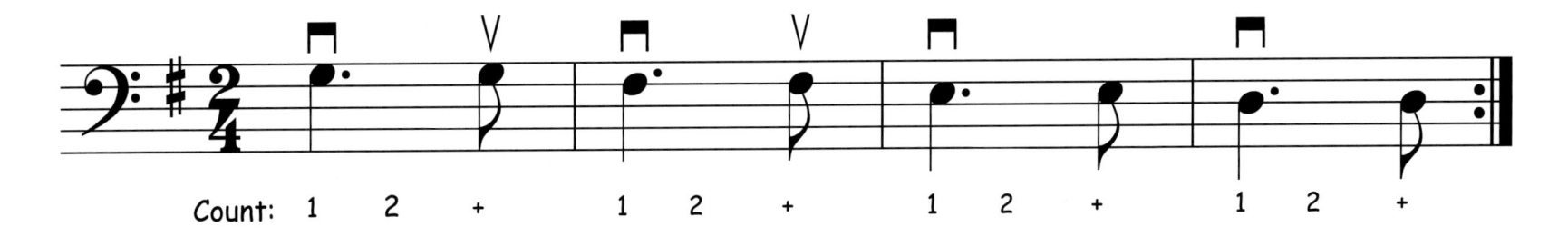

Count: 1   2   +   1   2   +   1   2   +   1   2   +

Dotted Notes

When a dot is placed after a note it makes the note half as long again.

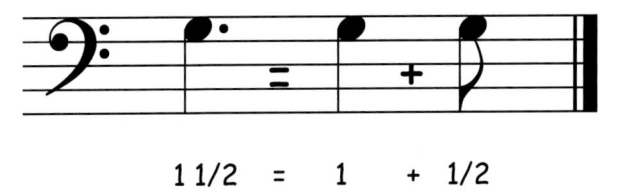

3   =   2   +   1

1 1/2   =   1   +   1/2

47

May Song

> means getting quieter.

< means getting louder.

First and Second Time Bars

The first part of this piece of music is repeated but
the fourth bar is different the second time it is played.
Play the first time bar the first time.
Skip this bar and play the second time bar on the repeat.
Leave out the repeat when you play the 'Da Capo'.

Hymn to Joy

Beethoven

The violins are learning to play the notes on their 'E' string. Listen as they play this familiar tune and notice how it sounds an octave higher than before. When they can play their new notes, play along with them, either using the tune on page 16, or the harmony part written below.
If you have no violin players in your group, you may skip this page.

The Giant's Lullaby

Harmony Part

Country Gardens

The violas and cellos are learning to play the notes on their 'C' string.
When they can play their new notes you can play this tune along with them.

Kumbayah

1. Name each note.
   Which finger do you use to play it?   **?**

2. Put in the barlines.

A New Rhythm

6 Quavers in the Bar

This time signature means that there are six beats in every bar. The figure 8 on the bottom of the time signature means that each beat is a quaver note.

In this rhythm the quavers 'hold hands' in groups of three.

Play and count.

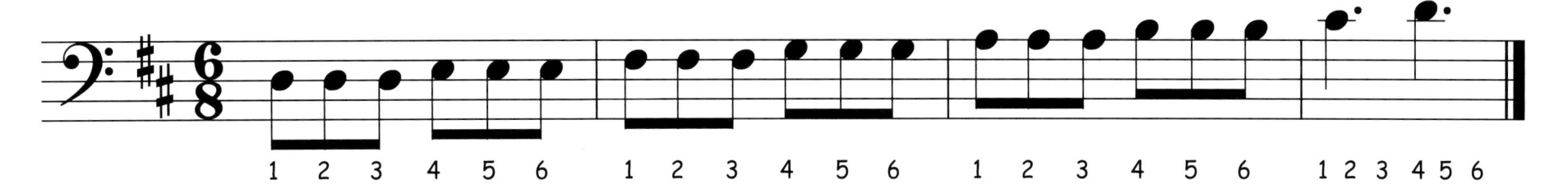

1 2 3   4 5 6   1 2 3   4 5 6   1 2 3   4 5 6   1 2 3 4 5 6

Remember, a crotchet is worth two quavers.

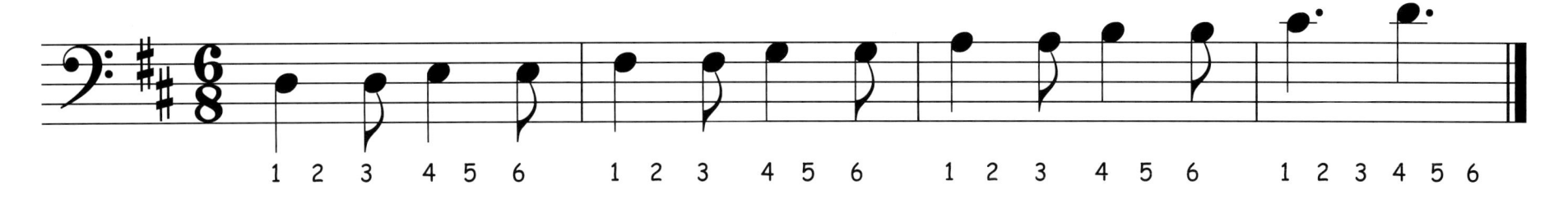

1 2 3   4 5 6   1 2 3   4 5 6   1 2 3   4 5 6   1 2 3 4 5 6

Often the 6/8 rhythm is counted as two ♩. beats in the bar.
Each beat has three quavers.

Play and count.

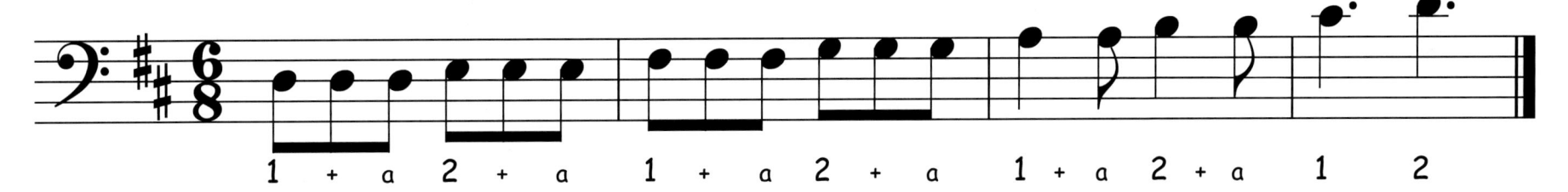

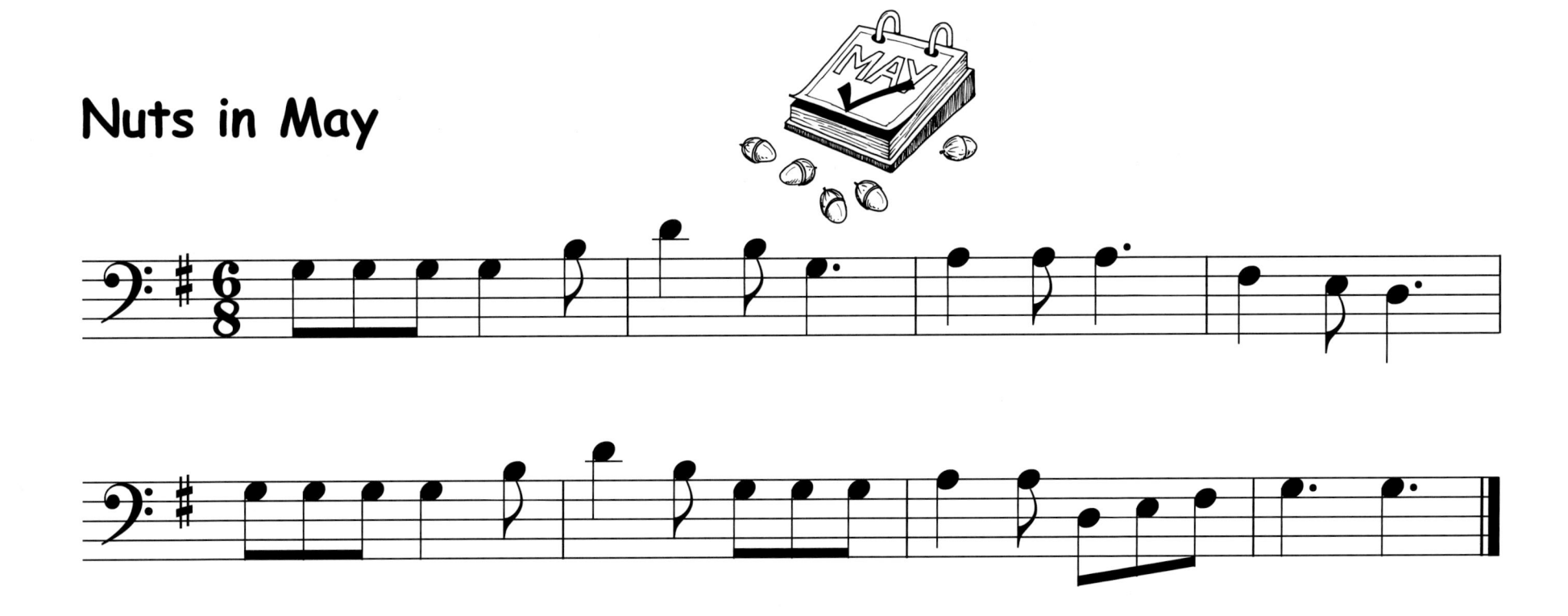

1 + a 2 + a 1 + a 2 + a 1 + a 2 + a 1   2

Nuts in May

Question Time

1. There is a note called 'B' in the fifth bar. How many beats does it get? ....

2. What is the name of the first note in bar three? ....

3. How many beats are there in each bar? ....

4. How long is the rest in bar two? ....

5. What scale or key is the piece of music in? ....

6. What is the interval between the first two notes? ....

7. If you were to play this tune on a piano,
   how many times would you play a black note? ....

Additional Repertoire

Can you play all of the 'Tricks' in the book? Then let's –

Dance and Sing around the World

Index

		page
Australia	Waltzing Matilda	58
England	Tallis's Canon	59
France	Il est Né	60
Germany	Hollahai	61
Greece	Provatakya	62
Holland	Clog Dance	63
Ireland	The Irish Washerwoman	64
Israel	Rhanouka	65
Scotland	Skye Boat Song	66
Switzerland	The Cuckoo	67
United States of America	Turkey in the Straw	68
West Indies	Mango Walk	69

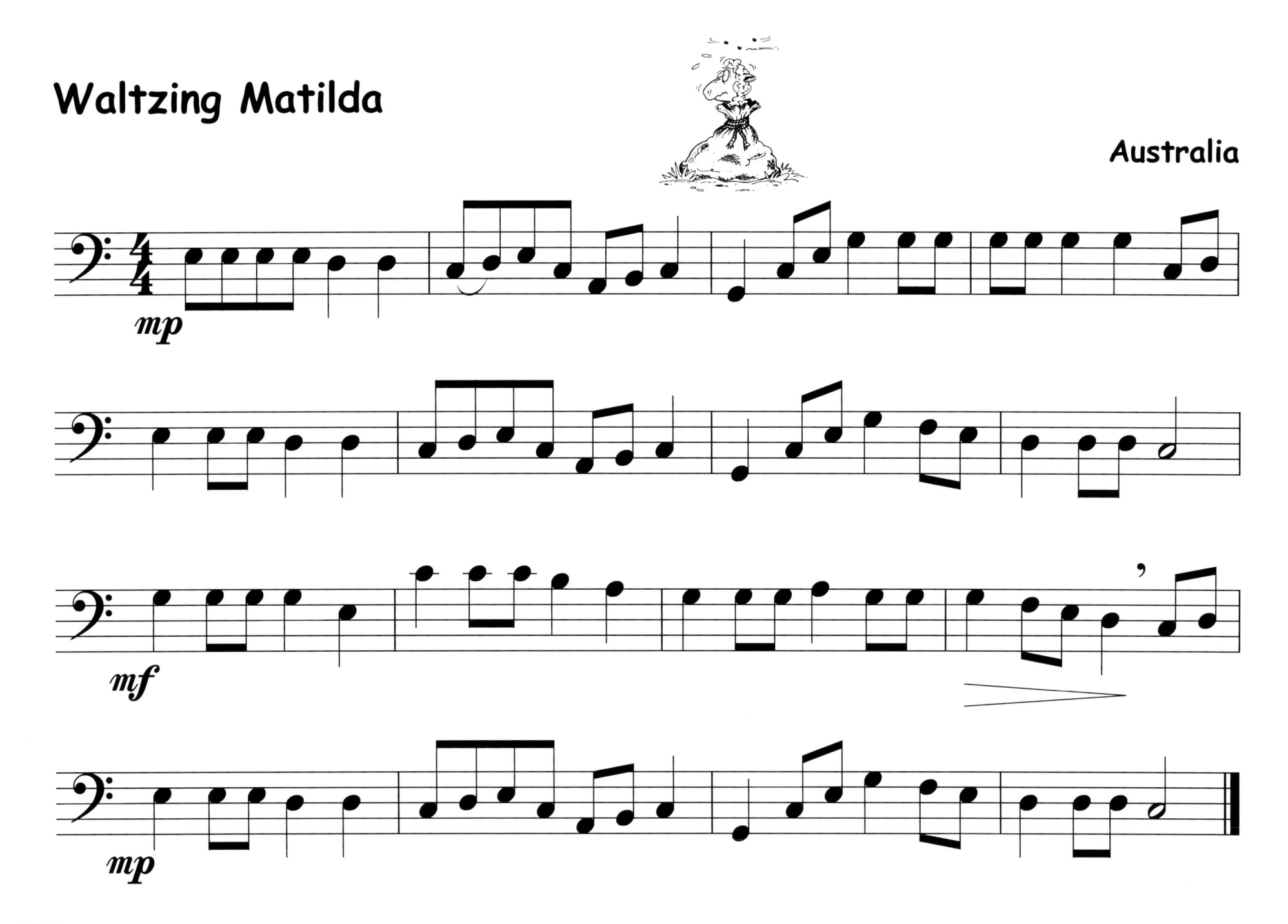

Waltzing Matilda

Australia

A **canon** in music is a type of round.
The second player starts when the first player reaches the number 2 in the music. Each player starts one bar (or four beats) after the other.

Tallis was an English composer who lived in the 16th century.
He wrote this canon in 1567 AD.

Tallis's Canon

England

This is a French Christmas song.

Il est Né

France

Hollahi

Germany

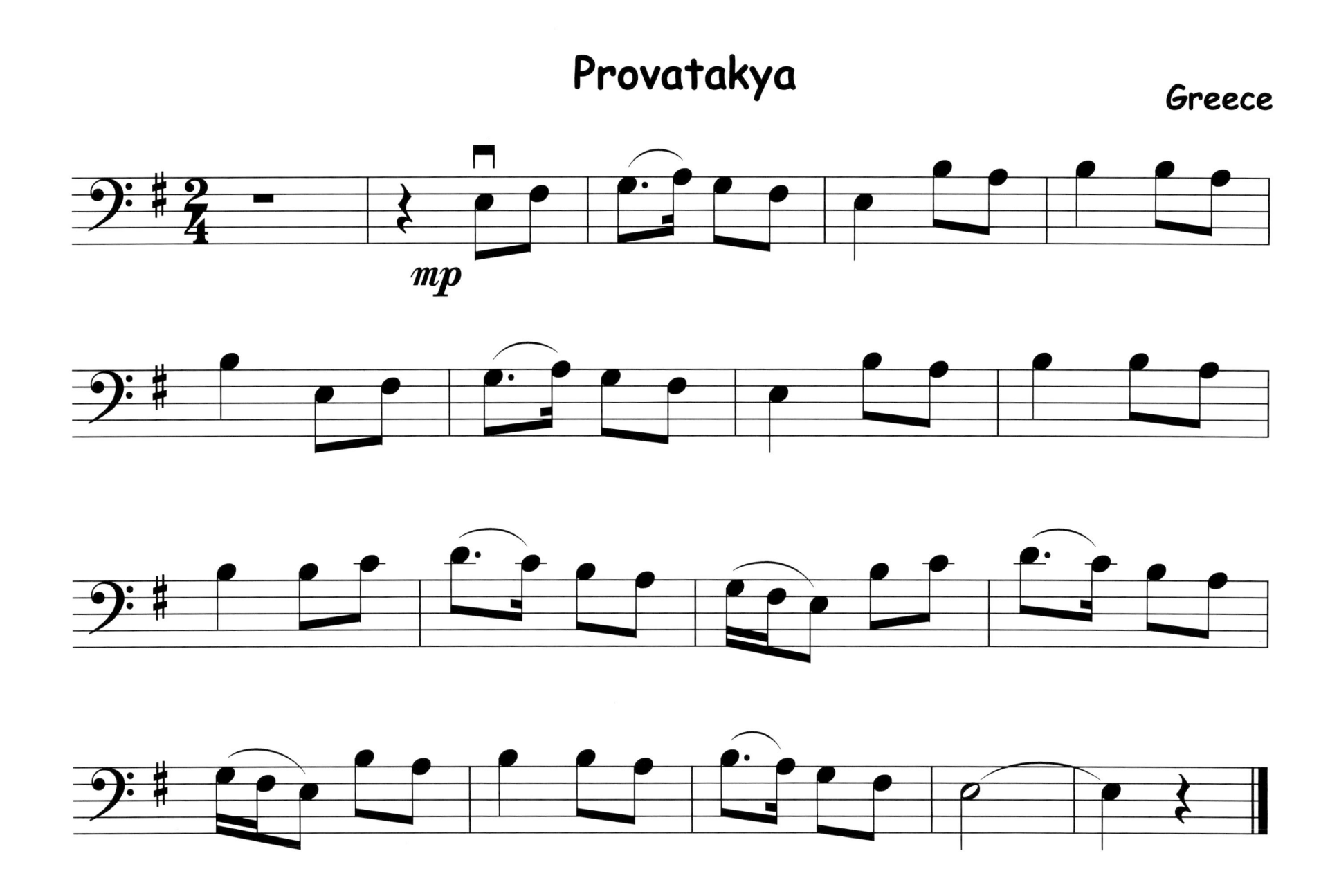

Provatakya

Greece

Clog Dance

Holland

The Irish Washerwoman

Ireland

Rhanouka

Israel

Skye Boat Song

Scotland

The Cuckoo

Switzerland

Turkey in the Straw

U.S.A.

Mango Walk

West Indies